COACHED BY PAUL THE APOSTLE

Lessons in Transformation

STUDY GUIDE

FR. NATHAN CROMLY

Scepter

SAINT JOHN INSTITUTE

Published by Scepter Publishers, Inc.

info@scepterpublishers.org

www.scepterpublishers.org

800-322-8773

New York

Cover illustration by Gordon Ross (1873-1946) from Living Biographies of Religious Leaders.

Text and cover design: Studio Red Design

Interior artwork: Brie Schulze at brieschulze.com

ISBN: (pbk) 978-1-59417-542-8

ISBN: (ebook) 978-1-59417-543-5

Printed in the United States of America

Contents

About This Study Guide

Origin and Purpose of This Study Guide

We can often think of saints as far-off figures—people to study and to ask for prayers from, but ultimately people who are far outside the realm of relatability. However, just as you face your daily struggles, the saints have struggled too. Saints even as grand as St. Paul have lived through the same fears you're living through. The difference is that, though the saints encountered those fears, they did not let those fears paralyze them. They offered those fears to Jesus Christ. And the good news: St. Paul shows us a way forward through our fears by the grace of God. Walking on that path—following Jesus—makes us his disciples and places us on a pathway to lead the world around us.

Coached by Paul aims to reveal these lessons to each reader. And as saints exist as part of a heavenly communion, this study guide aims to bring companions together in earthly communion to help each other apply the leadership lessons St. Paul teaches us in practical ways. Plus, this study guide offers tools to put into practice the ways St. Paul shows us to surrender our fears to Christ, so that together we can be people of action and influence our families, workplaces, and cultures for Christ.

Getting Organized

We've put together a structure to help your group grasp the practicality behind the ways in which St. Paul leads us toward the graces of God. Each gathering will focus on one chapter from *Coached by Paul* and follows this format:

Opening Prayer

- Pray the Prayer for the Year of St. Paul out loud, found on the inside back cover of the study guide . . .
- . . . or a volunteer can pray out loud a prayer from the heart.

Readings

- A volunteer(s) will read out loud the writings of St. Paul from the New Testament.
    - ◊ The three readings from the "Pondering with Paul" section at the end of each chapter in *Coached by Paul* are included in this guide.
    - ◊ It is left to the discretion of the group whether you like to read one reading or multiple readings. You can choose the reading(s) that speaks most to you.
- Take a moment of silence after the reading(s) to give the Word time to settle into your hearts.

Sharing

- The group shares any insights received from the chapter and the readings.

Coaching Convo

- The group will have the opportunity to apply St. Paul's coaching to a specific situation or situations from members of the group.
- If no one has a situation in which they would like to be coached, simply skip this section and move to the "Pondering with Paul" discussion questions.

"Pondering with Paul" Discussion Questions

- This section can be skipped if the Coaching Convo discussion runs long.
- The "Pondering with Paul" questions can be found at the end of each chapter in the book. Take some time to discuss how each group member responded to these questions.

Wrapping Up

- Share one takeaway from the group discussion.
- Share any relevant logistical information (announcements, time and location of the next gathering, and so forth).

Closing Prayer

- Members of the group ask for prayers for any petitions.
- Members of the group then pray the Our Father out loud together . . .
- . . . finishing with an appeal to St. Paul, asking, "St. Paul, pray for us."

Explanation of the Coaching Convo

Good coaching is only effective when put into practice by those being coached. Since this book is intended to be a practical guide to uniting faith and leadership, through the example set forth by St. Paul, we've set time aside in each gathering for the group to apply what they've learned to real life situations.

This conversation is intended to be different than sharing or discussion questions. Think of your fellow group members as your teammates—how can you encourage them to follow the example and teachings of your coach (St. Paul) to help them achieve victory (becoming an instrument in the hands of God, allowing God to influence the world through them)?

Don't worry about getting it perfect! Practice makes progress, and what is important is becoming more attuned to the Holy Spirit with the help of your teammates and St. Paul, your coach.

Best Practices

- Each member of the group should have a personal copy of *Coached by Paul* so that they can read the appropriate chapter ahead of each gathering.
- Begin and end each session in prayer.
    - ◊ We've included a prayer to St. Paul that can be used as an opening prayer, though the group may select a different prayer or pray from the heart.
    - ◊ It is strongly recommended that each gathering ends by praying the Lord's Prayer together, out loud as a group.

- Group members should be respectful to one another, and each member should be able to trust that, unless under extreme circumstances, information shared with the group is confidential.
    - ◊ If you disagree with something shared by a group member, look at that as an opportunity to take this to Jesus in prayer.
- Each group can personally decide how often to meet and for how long each gathering should last. This study guide can be used at any pace.
- It can be helpful for each group member to come with their own Bible.
- If journaling or note-taking is beneficial to a member, we recommend writing your inspirations down as you go.

Encouragement

Starting a small group of any kind can feel intimidating. Just like anything else, it requires a little more effort from us, and a little more time. That is why it is important for us to remember that we don't do a small group for ourselves alone; in fact, we do it for God and for the friends who can be helped by it along the way. Just like St. Paul the Apostle, who gathered people to hear God's word and find fellowship with one another in households and public spaces during his lifetime, we gather our friends to let God speak to us in our day.

You can do this! All we need to do is open the door to Jesus, create the possibility, invite our friends, and open our hearts. He will do the rest. "For where two or three are gathered in my name, there am I in the midst of them" (Mt. 18:20).

FIRST GATHERING

Coached by Paul

Introduction

"The heart of everything Paul teaches can be found in the wisdom of the Cross."

Opening Prayer

Choose a volunteer to open the gathering with prayer, either read for the group or from the heart. Prayer for the Year of St. Paul can be found on the inside back cover.

Readings

Acts 26

Agrippa said to Paul, "You have permission to speak for yourself." Then Paul stretched out his hand and made his defense:

"I think myself fortunate that it is before you, King Agrippa, I am to make my defense today against all the accusations of the Jews, because you are especially familiar with all customs and controversies of the Jews; therefore I beg you to listen to me patiently.

"My manner of life from my youth, spent from the beginning among my own nation and at Jerusalem, is known by all the Jews. They have known for a long time, if they are willing to testify, that according to the strictest party of our religion I have lived as a Pharisee. And now I stand here on trial for hope in the promise made by God to our fathers, to which our twelve tribes hope to attain, as they earnestly worship night and day. And for this hope I am accused by Jews, O king! Why is it thought incredible by any of you that God raises the dead?

"I myself was convinced that I ought to do many things in opposing the name of Jesus of Nazareth. And I did so in

Jerusalem; I not only shut up many of the saints in prison, by authority from the chief priests, but when they were put to death I cast my vote against them. And I punished them often in all the synagogues and tried to make them blaspheme; and in raging fury against them, I persecuted them even to foreign cities.

"Thus I journeyed to Damascus with the authority and commission of the chief priests. At midday, O king, I saw on the way a light from heaven, brighter than the sun, shining round me and those who journeyed with me. And when we had all fallen to the ground, I heard a voice saying to me in the Hebrew language, 'Saul, Saul, why do you persecute me? It hurts you to kick against the goads.' And I said, 'Who are you, Lord?' And the Lord said, 'I am Jesus whom you are persecuting. But rise and stand upon your feet; for I have appeared to you for this purpose, to appoint you to serve and bear witness to the things in which you have seen me and to those in which I will appear to you, delivering you from the people and from the Gentiles—to whom I send you to open their eyes, that they may turn from darkness to light and from the power of Satan to God, that they may receive forgiveness of sins and a place among those who are sanctified by faith in me.'

"Wherefore, O King Agrippa, I was not disobedient to the heavenly vision, but declared first to those at Damascus, then at Jerusalem and throughout all the country of Judea, and also to the Gentiles, that they should repent and turn to God and perform deeds worthy of their repentance. For this reason the Jews seized me in the temple and tried to kill me. To this day I have had the help that comes from God, and so I stand here testifying both to small and great, saying nothing but what the prophets and Moses said would come to pass: that the Christ must suffer, and that, by being the first to rise from the dead, he would proclaim light both to the people and to the Gentiles."

And as he thus made his defense, Festus said with a loud voice, "Paul, you are mad; your great learning is turning you mad." But Paul said, "I am not mad, most excellent Festus, but I am speaking the sober truth. For the king knows about these things, and to him I speak freely; for I am persuaded that none of these things has escaped his notice, for this was not done in a corner. King Agrippa, do you believe the prophets? I know that you believe." And Agrippa said to Paul, "In a short time you think to make me a Christian!" And Paul said, "Whether short or long, I would to God that not only you but also all who hear me this day might become such as I am—except for these chains."

Then the king rose, and the governor and Bernice and those who were sitting with them; and when they had withdrawn, they said to one another, "This man is doing nothing to deserve death or imprisonment." And Agrippa said to Festus, "This man could have been set free if he had not appealed to Caesar."

After the readings, take a moment of silence to allow the Word to settle into your hearts and to open your heart to the voice of the Holy Spirit.

Personal inspiration:

Sharing

Go around the room and, one by one, share what interested you about the group and what you'd like to get out of these coaching sessions. (It's OK to pass if desired.)

Personal insights:

> *Stat crux dum volvitur orbis: The world spins while the cross stands erect.*

Coaching Convo

Is there anyone in the group that needs help applying the lessons from this chapter to a situation in their life? After our volunteer shares their situation, spend time as a group, using St. Paul's coaching in this chapter, to provide helpful insight into this situation.

Personal struggle:

____

____

____

St. Paul's Condensed Coaching

Being a leader means influencing other people. Being a Christian leader, as St. Paul shows us, means bringing God's influence to other people. Christian leadership calls us to engage in love right where we are, in our current daily duties, rooted in the Cross of Jesus, and growing deeper in relationship with the One who made us.

Wrapping Up

Go around the room and, one by one, share an insight or lesson that you'll be taking away from this group conversation. (It's OK to pass if desired.)

For Next Time . . .

- Read *Coached by Paul the Apostle* Chapter 1: "Freedom's Roadmap."
- Reflect on the "Pondering with Paul" questions on page 30.

- Any other group announcements?
- Date, time, and place for the next gathering is

  ____.

Closing

Petitions

Members of the group share any petitions that they would like the group to pray for together.

Our Father

Pray the Our Father out loud together, finishing with an appeal to St. Paul:

"St. Paul, pray for us."

"Mundo inconcussa supersto: I stand unshaken over the world."

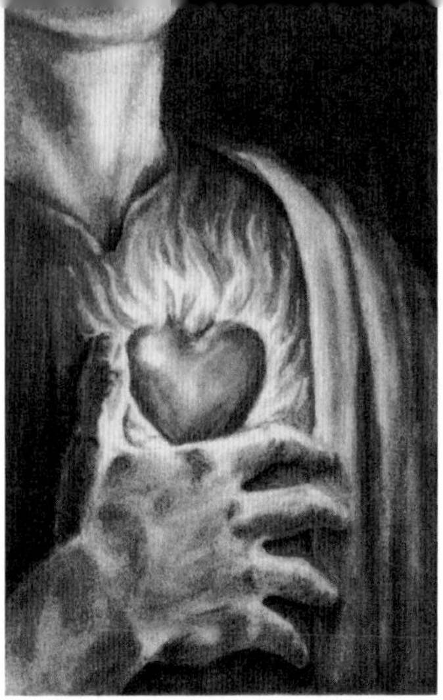

SECOND GATHERING

Coached by Paul Chapter 1

Freedom's Roadmap

"This is how St. Paul will coach us—through these five stages of action, in the midst of our fears, and into Christ's freedom."

Opening Prayer

Choose a volunteer to open the gathering with prayer, either read for the group or from the heart. Prayer for the Year of St. Paul can be found on the inside back cover.

Readings

Choose one to three volunteers to read one or more of the Scriptures below out loud.

1 Timothy 6:2–16

Those who have believing masters must not be disrespectful on the ground that they are brethren; rather they must serve all the better since those who benefit by their service are believers and beloved.

Teach and urge these duties. If any one teaches otherwise and does not agree with the sound words of our Lord Jesus Christ and the teaching which accords with godliness, he is puffed up with conceit, he knows nothing; he has a morbid craving for controversy and for disputes about words, which produce envy, dissension, slander, base suspicions, and wrangling among men who are depraved in mind and bereft of the truth, imagining that godliness is a means of gain. There is great gain in godliness with contentment; for we brought nothing into the world, and we cannot take anything out of the world; but if we have food and clothing, with these we shall be content. But those who desire to be rich fall into temptation, into a snare, into many senseless and hurtful desires that plunge men into ruin and destruction. For the love of money is the root of all evils; it is through this craving that some have wandered away from the faith and pierced their hearts with many pangs.

But as for you, man of God, shun all this; aim at righteousness, godliness, faith, love, steadfastness, gentleness. Fight the good fight of the faith; take hold of the eternal life to which you were called when you made the good confession in the presence of many witnesses. In the presence of God who gives life to all things, and of Christ Jesus who in his testimony before Pontius Pilate made the good confession, I charge you to keep the commandment unstained and free from reproach until the appearing of our Lord Jesus Christ; and this will be made manifest at the proper time by the blessed and only Sovereign, the King of kings and Lord of lords, who alone has immortality and dwells in unapproachable light, whom no man has ever seen or can see. To him be honor and eternal dominion. Amen.

Philippians 2:12–18

Therefore, my beloved, as you have always obeyed, so now, not only as in my presence but much more in my absence, work out your own salvation with fear and trembling; for God is at work in you, both to will and to work for his good pleasure.

Do all things without grumbling or questioning, that you may be blameless and innocent, children of God without blemish in the midst of a crooked and perverse generation, among whom you shine as lights in the world, holding fast the word of life, so that in the day of Christ I may be proud that I did not run in vain or labor in vain. Even if I am to be poured as a libation upon the sacrificial offering of your faith, I am glad and rejoice with you all. Likewise you also should be glad and rejoice with me.

Romans 8:12–37

So then, brethren, we are debtors, not to the flesh, to live according to the flesh—for if you live according to the flesh you will die, but if by the Spirit you put to death the deeds of the body you will live. For all who are led by the Spirit of God are sons of God. For you did not receive the spirit of slavery to fall back into fear, but you have received the spirit of sonship. When we cry, "Abba! Father!" it is the Spirit himself bearing witness with our spirit that we are children of God, and if children, then heirs, heirs of God and fellow heirs with Christ, provided we suffer with him in order that we may also be glorified with him.

I consider that the sufferings of this present time are not worth comparing with the glory that is to be revealed to us. For the creation waits with eager longing for the revealing of the sons of God; for the creation was subjected to futility, not of its own will but by the will of him who subjected it in hope; because the creation itself will be set free from its bondage to decay and obtain the glorious liberty of the children of God. We know that the whole creation has been groaning in travail together until now; and not only the creation, but we ourselves, who have the first fruits of the Spirit, groan inwardly as we wait for adoption as sons, the redemption of our bodies. For in this hope we were saved. Now hope that is seen is not hope. For who hopes for what he sees? But if we hope for what we do not see, we wait for it with patience.

Likewise the Spirit helps us in our weakness; for we do not know how to pray as we ought, but the Spirit himself intercedes for us with sighs too deep for words. And he who searches the hearts of men knows what is the mind of the Spirit, because the Spirit intercedes for the saints according to the will of God.

We know that in everything God works for good with those who love him, who are called according to his purpose. For those whom he foreknew he also predestined to be conformed to the image of his Son, in order that he might be the first-born among many brethren. And those whom he predestined he also called; and those whom he called he also justified; and those whom he justified he also glorified.

What then shall we say to this? If God is for us, who is against us? He who did not spare his own Son but gave him up for us all, will he not also give us all things with him? Who shall bring any charge against God's elect? It is God who justifies; who is to condemn? Is it Christ Jesus, who died, yes, who was raised from the dead, who is at the right hand of God, who indeed intercedes for us? Who shall separate us from the love of Christ? Shall tribulation, or distress, or persecution, or famine, or nakedness, or peril, or sword? As it is written, "For thy sake we are being killed all the day long; we are regarded as sheep to be slaughtered." No, in all these things we are more than conquerors through him who loved us.

After the readings, take a moment of silence to allow the Word to settle into your hearts and to open your heart to the voice of the Holy Spirit.

Personal inspiration:

Sharing

Go around the room and, one by one, share an insight or lesson that was revealed to you from this chapter. (It's OK to pass if desired.)

Personal insights:

> *Do we know* why *we are doing what we are doing?*

Coaching Convo

Is there anyone in the group that needs help applying the lessons from this chapter to a situation in their life? Spend time as a group, using St. Paul's coaching in this chapter, to provide insight into this situation.

Personal struggle:

____

____

____

St. Paul's Condensed Coaching

"Whenever we do something intentionally, whether great or small, we engage our freedom. And this means we necessarily pass through five stages:

1. We start by wanting to do something.
    a. What is the good that I want to pursue?
    b. Here, the pitfall of Fatalism can be met by God's grace of Christian Creativity.
2. We decide on the best way to do it.
    a. What is the best way for me to obtain it?
    b. Here, the pitfall of Fog can be met by God's grace of Christian Clarity.
3. We choose to begin to do it . . . What are the first steps I need to take?
    a. Here, the pitfall of Flight can be met by God's grace of Christian Courage.

4. And we discover how to finish what we started.
    a. How can I persevere in my pursuit, despite whatever struggles I encounter?
    b. Here, the pitfall of Fatigue can be met by God's grace of Christian Constancy.
5. Finally, we find a way to share with others what we have done so that they can be a part of it.
    a. What is the best way to share what I am doing with others so that they can be a part of it?
    b. Here, the pitfall of Forlornness can be met by God's grace of Christian Communion.

"Pondering with Paul" Discussion Questions

Questions are found on p. 30 of the book.

Wrapping Up

Go around the room and, one by one, share an insight or lesson that you'll be taking away from this group conversation. (It's OK to pass if desired.)

For Next Time . . .

- Read *Coached by Paul the Apostle* Chapter 2: "With Eyes like Flames of Fire."
- Reflect on the "Pondering with Paul" questions on page 45.
- Any other group announcements?
- Date, time, and place for the next gathering is ______________________________.

Closing

Petitions

Members of the group share any petitions that they would like the group to pray for together.

Our Father

Pray the Our Father out loud together, finishing with an appeal to St. Paul:

"St. Paul, pray for us."

> ***A life lived in freedom is never boring.*** *Faith awakens the sleeping giant of our heart. We discover who we are*—***and who we are not***—*when we finally test ourselves against the demands of true love.*

THIRD GATHERING

Coached by Paul Chapter 2

With Eyes like Flames of Fire

"*. . . when it comes to our lives as human beings on this earth, God is not a big fan of the status quo.*"

Opening Prayer

Choose a volunteer to open the gathering with prayer, either read for the group or from the heart. Prayer for the Year of St. Paul can be found on the inside back cover.

Readings

Choose one to three volunteers to read one or more of the Scriptures below out loud.

Romans 12:1–2

I appeal to you therefore, brethren, by the mercies of God, to present your bodies as a living sacrifice, holy and acceptable to God, which is your spiritual worship. Do not be conformed to this world but be transformed by the renewal of your mind, that you may prove what is the will of God, what is good and acceptable and perfect.

Romans 5:6–6:23

While we were yet helpless, at the right time Christ died for the ungodly. Why, one will hardly die for a righteous man—though perhaps for a good man one will dare even to die. But God shows his love for us in that while we were yet sinners Christ died for us. Since, therefore, we are now justified by his blood, much more shall we be saved by him from the wrath of God. For if while we were enemies we were reconciled to God by the death of his Son, much more, now that we are reconciled, shall we be saved by his life. Not only so, but we also rejoice in God through our Lord Jesus Christ, through whom we have now received our reconciliation.

Therefore as sin came into the world through one man and death through sin, and so death spread to all men because all men sinned—sin indeed was in the world before the law was given, but sin is not counted where there is no law. Yet death reigned from Adam to Moses, even over those whose sins were not like the transgression of Adam, who was a type of the one who was to come.

But the free gift is not like the trespass. For if many died through one man's trespass, much more have the grace of God and the free gift in the grace of that one man Jesus Christ abounded for many. And the free gift is not like the effect of that one man's sin. For the judgment following one trespass brought condemnation, but the free gift following many trespasses brings justification. If, because of one man's trespass, death reigned through that one man, much more will those who receive the abundance of grace and the free gift of righteousness reign in life through the one man Jesus Christ.

Then as one man's trespass led to condemnation for all men, so one man's act of righteousness leads to acquittal and life for all men. For as by one man's disobedience many were made sinners, so by one man's obedience many will be made righteous. Law came in, to increase the trespass; but where sin increased, grace abounded all the more, so that, as sin reigned in death, grace also might reign through righteousness to eternal life through Jesus Christ our Lord.

What shall we say then? Are we to continue in sin that grace may abound? By no means! How can we who died to sin still live in it? Do you not know that all of us who have been baptized into Christ Jesus were baptized into his death? We were buried therefore with him by baptism into death, so that as Christ was raised from the dead by the glory of the Father, we too might walk in newness of life.

For if we have been united with him in a death like his, we shall certainly be united with him in a resurrection like his. We know that our old self was crucified with him so that the sinful body might be destroyed, and we might no longer be enslaved to sin. For he who has died is freed from sin. But if we have died with Christ, we believe that we shall also live with him. For we know that Christ being raised from the dead will never die again; death no longer has dominion over him. The death he died he died to sin, once for all, but the life he lives he lives to God. So you also must consider yourselves dead to sin and alive to God in Christ Jesus.

Let not sin therefore reign in your mortal bodies, to make you obey their passions. Do not yield your members to sin as instruments of wickedness, but yield yourselves to God as men who have been brought from death to life, and your members to God as instruments of righteousness. For sin will have no dominion over you, since you are not under law but under grace.

What then? Are we to sin because we are not under law but under grace? By no means! [Do you not know that if you yield yourselves to any one as obedient slaves, you are slaves of the one whom you obey, either of sin, which leads to death, or of obedience, which leads to righteousness? But thanks be to God, that you who were once slaves of sin have become obedient from the heart to the standard of teaching to which you were committed, and, having been set free from sin, have become slaves of righteousness. I am speaking in human terms, because of your natural limitations. For just as you once yielded your members to impurity and to greater and greater iniquity, so now yield your members to righteousness for sanctification.

When you were slaves of sin, you were free in regard to righteousness. But then what return did you get from the things of which you are now ashamed? The end of those things is death. But now that you have been set free from sin and have become slaves of God, the return you get is sanctification and its end, eternal life. For the wages of sin is death, but the free gift of God is eternal life in Christ Jesus our Lord.

Philippians 1:18–30
What then? Only that in every way, whether in pretense or in truth, Christ is proclaimed; and in that I rejoice.

Yes, and I shall rejoice. For I know that through your prayers and the help of the Spirit of Jesus Christ this will turn out for my deliverance, as it is my eager expectation and hope that I shall not be at all ashamed, but that with full courage now as always Christ will be honored in my body, whether by life or by death. For to me to live is Christ, and to die is gain. If it is to be life in the flesh, that means fruitful labor for me. Yet which I shall choose I cannot tell. I am hard pressed between the two. My desire is to depart and be with Christ, for that is far better. But to remain in the flesh is more necessary on your account. Convinced of this, I know that I shall remain and continue with you all, for your progress and joy in the faith, so that in me you may have ample cause to glory in Christ Jesus, because of my coming to you again.

Only let your manner of life be worthy of the gospel of Christ, so that whether I come and see you or am absent, I may hear of you that you stand firm in one spirit, with one mind striving side by side for the faith of the gospel, and not frightened in anything by your opponents. This is a clear omen to them of their destruction, but of your salvation, and that from God. For it has been granted to you that for the sake of Christ you should not only believe in him but also suffer for his sake, engaged in the same conflict which you saw and now hear to be mine.

After the readings, take a moment of silence to allow the Word to settle into your hearts and to open your heart to the voice of the Holy Spirit.

Personal inspiration:

Sharing

Go around the room and, one by one, share an insight or lesson that was revealed to you from this chapter. (It's OK to pass if desired.)

Personal insights:

Coaching Convo

Is there anyone in the group that needs help applying the lessons from this chapter to a situation in their life? Spend time as a group, using St. Paul's coaching in this chapter, to provide insight into this situation.

Personal struggle:

St. Paul's Condensed Coaching

Practical Lessons about how God works in us, shown by the life of St. Paul:

1. God usually wants to transform the world outside of us by transforming the world within us.
2. The conversion of St. Paul startles any sense we may have of our own unworthiness.
3. God does not do anything randomly or without intention . . . when God transforms us, he shapes us into the image of Jesus, his Son.

"Pondering with Paul" Questions for Discussion

Questions are found on p. 45 of the book.

Wrapping Up

Go around the room and, one by one, share an insight or lesson that you'll be taking away from this group conversation. (It's OK to pass if desired.)

For Next Time . . .

- Read *Coached by Paul the Apostle* Chapter 3: "Hold Your Head High."
- Reflect on the "Pondering with Paul" questions on page 63.
- Any other group announcements?
- Date, time, and place for the next gathering is ______________________________.

Closing

Petitions

Members of the group share any petitions that they would like the group to pray for together.

Our Father

Pray the Our Father out loud together, finishing with an appeal to St. Paul:

"St. Paul, pray for us."

> *"...our time on earth is one of constant transformation in the hands of God."*

FOURTH GATHERING

Coached by Paul Chapter 3

Hold Your Head High

"In the life of St. Paul, we see the power of a heart that is free. What was his secret? What made him tick?"

Opening Prayer

Choose a volunteer to open the gathering with prayer, either read for the group or from the heart. Prayer for the Year of St. Paul can be found on the inside back cover.

Readings

Choose one to three volunteers to read one or more of the Scriptures below out loud.

Romans 12:3–8

For by the grace given to me I bid every one among you not to think of himself more highly than he ought to think, but to think with sober judgment, each according to the measure of faith which God has assigned him. For as in one body we have many members, and all the members do not have the same function, so we, though many, are one body in Christ, and individually members one of another. Having gifts that differ according to the grace given to us, let us use them: if prophecy, in proportion to our faith; if service, in our serving; he who teaches, in his teaching; he who exhorts, in his exhortation; he who contributes, in liberality; he who gives aid, with zeal; he who does acts of mercy, with cheerfulness.

---

2 Corinthians 12:1–10

I must boast; there is nothing to be gained by it, but I will go on to visions and revelations of the Lord. I know a man in Christ who fourteen years ago was caught up to the third heaven—whether in the body or out of the body I do not know, God knows. And I know that this man was caught up into Paradise—whether in the body or out of the body I do not know, God knows—and he heard things that cannot be told, which man may not utter. On behalf of this man I will boast, but on my own behalf I will not boast, except of my weaknesses. Though if I wish to boast, I shall not be a fool, for I shall be speaking the truth. But I refrain from it, so that no one may think more of me than he sees in me or hears from me. And to keep me from being too elated by the abundance of revelations, a thorn was given me in the flesh, a messenger of Satan, to harass me, to keep me from being too elated. Three times I besought the Lord about this, that it should leave me; but he said to me, "My grace is sufficient for you, for my power is made perfect in weakness." I will all the more gladly boast of my weaknesses, that the power of Christ may rest upon me. For the sake of Christ, then, I am content with weaknesses, insults, hardships, persecutions, and calamities; for when I am weak, then I am strong.

---

2 Corinthians 1:18–24

As surely as God is faithful, our word to you has not been Yes and No. For the Son of God, Jesus Christ, whom we preached among you, Silvanus and Timothy and I, was not Yes and No; but in him it is always Yes. For all the promises of God find their Yes in him. That is why we utter the Amen through him, to the glory of God. But it is God who establishes us with you in Christ, and has commissioned us; he has put his seal upon us and given us his Spirit in our hearts as a guarantee.

But I call God to witness against me—it was to spare you that I refrained from coming to Corinth. Not that we lord it over your faith; we work with you for your joy, for you stand firm in your faith.

After the readings, take a moment of silence to allow the Word to settle into your hearts and to open your heart to the voice of the Holy Spirit.

Personal inspiration:

"...God makes us free to respond to our weaknesses with the courage that leads to holiness instead of the cowardice that leads to sin."

Sharing

Go around the room and, one by one, share an insight or lesson that was revealed to you from this chapter. (It's OK to pass if desired.)

Personal insights:

____

____

____

Coaching Convo

Is there anyone in the group that needs help applying the lessons from this chapter to a situation in their life? Spend time as a group, using St. Paul's coaching in this chapter, to provide insight into this situation.

Personal struggle:

____

____

____

St. Paul's Condensed Coaching

Throughout his life, St. Paul coaches us that God entrusts us all with a unique mission. Though at times we may feel weak, unable to believe our own will can carry us, St. Paul demonstrates that in these very moments we can "hold our head high" because it is here where Christ meets us and becomes the strength in our weakness. Christian

Courage does not mean the absence of fear, but, instead, following God despite our fears.

"Pondering with Paul" Discussion Questions

Questions are found on p. 63 of the book.

Wrapping Up

Go around the room and, one by one, share an insight or lesson that you'll be taking away from this group conversation. (It's OK to pass if desired.)

For Next Time . . .

- Read *Coached by Paul the Apostle* Chapter 4: "In Ashes, Flame."
- Reflect on the "Pondering with Paul" questions on page 82.
- Any other group announcements?
- Date, time, and place for the next gathering is
  ____.

Closing

Petitions

Members of the group share any petitions that they would like the group to pray for together.

Our Father

Pray the Our Father out loud together, finishing with an appeal to St. Paul:

"St. Paul, pray for us."

"It takes courage to try to act in love when we keenly feel our incapacity to do so."

FIFTH GATHERING

Coached by Paul Chapter 4

In Ashes, Flame

The ashes of [Paul's] past would remain; God did not need to remove them from him to start his fire.

Opening Prayer

Choose a volunteer to open the gathering with prayer, either read for the group or from the heart. Prayer for the Year of St. Paul can be found on the inside back cover.

Readings

Choose one to three volunteers to read one or more of the Scriptures below out loud.

Acts 16:16–39

As we were going to the place of prayer, we were met by a slave girl who had a spirit of divination and brought her owners much gain by soothsaying. She followed Paul and us, crying, "These men are servants of the Most High God, who proclaim to you the way of salvation." And this she did for many days. But Paul was annoyed, and turned and said to the spirit, "I charge you in the name of Jesus Christ to come out of her." And it came out that very hour.

But when her owners saw that their hope of gain was gone, they seized Paul and Silas and dragged them into the market place before the rulers; and when they had brought them to the magistrates they said, "These men are Jews and they are disturbing our city. They advocate customs which it is not lawful for us Romans to accept or practice." The crowd joined in attacking them; and the magistrates tore the garments off them and gave orders to beat them with rods. And when they had inflicted many blows upon them, they threw them into prison, charging the jailer to keep them safely. Having received this charge, he put them into the inner prison and fastened their feet in the stocks.

But about midnight Paul and Silas were praying and singing hymns to God, and the prisoners were listening to them, and suddenly there was a great earthquake, so that the foundations of the prison were shaken; and immediately all the doors were opened and every one's fetters were unfastened. When the jailer woke and saw that the prison doors were open, he drew his sword and was about to kill himself, supposing that the prisoners had escaped. But Paul cried with a loud voice, "Do not harm yourself, for we are all here." And he called for lights and rushed in, and trembling with fear he fell down before Paul and Silas, and brought them out and said, "Men, what must I do to be saved?" And they said, "Believe in the Lord Jesus, and you will be saved, you and your household." And they spoke the word of the Lord to him and to all that were in his house. And he took them the same hour of the night, and washed their wounds, and he was baptized at once, with all his family. Then he brought them up into his house, and set food before them; and he rejoiced with all his household that he had believed in God.

But when it was day, the magistrates sent the police, saying, "Let those men go." And the jailer reported the words to Paul, saying, "The magistrates have sent to let you go; now therefore come out and go in peace." But Paul said to them, "They have beaten us publicly, uncondemned, men who are Roman citizens, and have thrown us into prison; and do they now cast us out secretly? No! let them come themselves and take us out." The police reported these words to the magistrates, and they were afraid when they heard that they were Roman citizens; so they came and apologized to them. And they took them out and asked them to leave the city.

---

2 Corinthians 5:17–21

Therefore, if any one is in Christ, he is a new creation; the old has passed away, behold, the new has come. All this is from God, who through Christ reconciled us to himself and gave us the ministry of reconciliation; that is, God was in Christ reconciling the world to himself, not counting their trespasses against them, and entrusting to us the message of reconciliation. So we are ambassadors for Christ, God making his appeal through us. We beseech you on behalf of Christ, be reconciled to God. For our sake he made him to be sin who knew no sin, so that in him we might become the righteousness of God.

---

1 Corinthians 15:50–58

I tell you this, brethren: flesh and blood cannot inherit the kingdom of God, nor does the perishable inherit the imperishable.

Lo! I tell you a mystery. We shall not all sleep, but we shall all be changed, in a moment, in the twinkling of an eye, at the last trumpet. For the trumpet will sound, and the dead will be raised imperishable, and we shall be changed. For this perishable nature must put on the imperishable, and this mortal nature must put on immortality. When the perishable puts on the imperishable, and the mortal puts on immortality, then shall come to pass the saying that is written:

"Death is swallowed up in victory."

"O death, where is thy victory?

O death, where is thy sting?"

The sting of death is sin, and the power of sin is the law. But thanks be to God, who gives us the victory through our Lord Jesus Christ.

Therefore, my beloved brethren, be steadfast, immovable, always abounding in the work of the Lord, knowing that in the Lord your labor is not in vain.

After the readings, take a moment of silence to allow the Word to settle into your hearts and to open your heart to the voice of the Holy Spirit.

Personal inspiration:

Sharing

Go around the room and, one by one, share an insight or lesson that was revealed to you from this chapter. (It's OK to pass if desired.)

Personal insights:

____

____

____

Coaching Convo

Is there anyone in the group that needs help applying the lessons from this chapter to a situation in their life? Spend time as a group, using St. Paul's coaching in this chapter, to provide insight into this situation.

Personal struggle:

____

____

____

> *"…[Saint Paul] allowed his faith in the creative power of God's love to be the lens through which he looked at the world."*

St. Paul's Condensed Coaching

Fatalism tells us that there is no reason to try to do something because our actions are bound to be fruitless. St. Paul coaches us to keep alive the flame of Christian Creativity by placing our hope in a God that is always ready to do new things in our lives. When we do this, and have the courage to try to effectuate change, even in situations that seem hopeless to us, we allow God to do something new and wonderful.

"Pondering with Paul" Discussion Questions

Questions are found on p. 82 of the book.

Wrapping Up

Go around the room and, one by one, share an insight or lesson that you'll be taking away from this group conversation. (It's OK to pass if desired.)

For Next Time . . .

- Read *Coached by Paul the Apostle* Chapter 5: "In Darkness, Light."
- Reflect on the "Pondering with Paul" questions on page 100.
- Any other group announcements?
- Date, time, and place for the next gathering is ____ .

Closing

Petitions

Members of the group share any petitions that they would like the group to pray for together.

Our Father

Pray the Our Father out loud together, finishing with an appeal to St. Paul:

"St. Paul, pray for us."

"What would our lives look like if we chose to light the candle of faith in the gloom that surrounds us instead of cursing the ambient darkness?"

SIXTH GATHERING

Coached by Paul Chapter 5

In Darkness, Light

If life were a trip to the grocery store, "fog" would make us circle the aisles for hours only to come back with an empty grocery cart!

Opening Prayer

Choose a volunteer to open the gathering with prayer, either read for the group or from the heart. Prayer for the Year of St. Paul can be found on the inside back cover.

Readings

Choose one to three volunteers to read one or more of the Scriptures below out loud.

1 Corinthians 2:6–10

Yet among the mature we do impart wisdom, although it is not a wisdom of this age or of the rulers of this age, who are doomed to pass away. But we impart a secret and hidden wisdom of God, which God decreed before the ages for our glorification. None of the rulers of this age understood this; for if they had, they would not have crucified the Lord of glory. But, as it is written,

"What no eye has seen, nor ear heard,

nor the heart of man conceived,

what God has prepared for those who love him,"

God has revealed to us through the Spirit. For the Spirit searches everything, even the depths of God.

Acts 16:6–10

And they went through the region of Phrygia and Galatia, having been forbidden by the Holy Spirit to speak the word in

Asia. And when they had come opposite Mysia, they attempted to go into Bithynia, but the Spirit of Jesus did not allow them; so, passing by Mysia, they went down to Troas. And a vision appeared to Paul in the night: a man of Macedonia was standing beseeching him and saying, “Come over to Macedonia and help us.” And when he had seen the vision, immediately we sought to go on into Macedonia, concluding that God had called us to preach the gospel to them.

Romans 8:12–17

So then, brethren, we are debtors, not to the flesh, to live according to the flesh—for if you live according to the flesh you will die, but if by the Spirit you put to death the deeds of the body you will live. For all who are led by the Spirit of God are sons of God. For you did not receive the spirit of slavery to fall back into fear, but you have received the spirit of sonship. When we cry, “Abba! Father!” it is the Spirit himself bearing witness with our spirit that we are children of God, and if children, then heirs, heirs of God and fellow heirs with Christ, provided we suffer with him in order that we may also be glorified with him.

After the readings, take a moment of silence to allow the Word to settle into your hearts and to open your heart to the voice of the Holy Spirit.

Personal inspiration:

Sharing

Go around the room and, one by one, share an insight or lesson that was revealed to you from this chapter. (It's OK to pass if desired.)

Personal insights:

Coaching Convo

Is there anyone in the group that needs help applying the lessons from this chapter to a situation in their life? Spend time as a group, using St. Paul's coaching in this chapter, to provide insight into this situation.

Personal struggle:

St. Paul's Condensed Coaching

Fog paralyses us when we're not able to discern the best way to act. What's the right choice? St. Paul coaches us that the Holy Spirit always knows the way, and with Christian Clarity, as long as we take the next step forward, he will direct those steps with certainty to work out his will.

"Pondering with Paul" Discussion Questions

Questions are found on p. 100 of the book.

Wrapping Up

Go around the room and, one by one, share an insight or lesson that you'll be taking away from this group conversation. (It's OK to pass if desired.)

For Next Time . . .

- Read *Coached by Paul the Apostle* Chapter 6: "Jumping."
- Reflect on the "Pondering with Paul" questions on page 115.
- Any other group announcements?
- Date, time, and place for the next gathering is ____ .

"Having problems with the problem,
that's the real problem!"

Closing

Petitions

Members of the group share any petitions that they would like the group to pray for together.

Our Father

Pray the Our Father out loud together, finishing with an appeal to St. Paul:

"St. Paul, pray for us."

"It's almost as if the Holy Spirit is not afraid of our errors or our poor decisions."

SEVENTH GATHERING

Coached by Paul Chapter 6

Jumping

"...jumping also means falling, and falling means being terrified for a brief moment, and being terrified for a brief moment is not exactly your definition of fun!"

Opening Prayer

Choose a volunteer to open the gathering with prayer, either read for the group or from the heart. Prayer for the Year of St. Paul can be found on the inside back cover.

Readings

Choose one to three volunteers to read one or more of the Scriptures below out loud.

Acts 13:1–4

Now in the church at Antioch there were prophets and teachers, Barnabas, Symeon who was called Niger, Lucius of Cyrene, Manaen a member of the court of Herod the tetrarch, and Saul. While they were worshiping the Lord and fasting, the Holy Spirit said, "Set apart for me Barnabas and Saul for the work to which I have called them." Then after fasting and praying they laid their hands on them and sent them off.

So, being sent out by the Holy Spirit, they went down to Seleucia; and from there they sailed to Cyprus.

Acts 18:1–11

After this he left Athens and went to Corinth. And he found a Jew named Aquila, a native of Pontus, lately come from Italy with his wife Priscilla, because Claudius had commanded all the Jews to leave Rome. And he went to see them; and because he was of the same trade he stayed with them, and they worked, for by trade they were tentmakers. And he argued in the synagogue every sabbath, and persuaded Jews and Greeks.

When Silas and Timothy arrived from Macedonia, Paul was occupied with preaching, testifying to the Jews that the Christ was Jesus. And when they opposed and reviled him, he shook out his garments and said to them, "Your blood be upon your heads! I am innocent. From now on I will go to the Gentiles." And he left there and went to the house of a man named Titius Justus, a worshiper of God; his house was next door to the synagogue. Crispus, the ruler of the synagogue, believed in the Lord, together with all his household; and many of the Corinthians hearing Paul believed and were baptized. And the Lord said to Paul one night in a vision, "Do not be afraid, but speak and do not be silent; for I am with you, and no man shall attack you to harm you; for I have many people in this city." And he stayed a year and six months, teaching the word of God among them.

Acts 22:30–23:11

But on the morrow, desiring to know the real reason why the Jews accused him, he unbound him, and commanded the chief priests and all the council to meet, and he brought Paul down and set him before them.

And Paul, looking intently at the council, said, "Brethren, I have lived before God in all good conscience up to this day."

And the high priest Ananias commanded those who stood by him to strike him on the mouth. Then Paul said to him, "God shall strike you, you whitewashed wall! Are you sitting to judge me according to the law, and yet contrary to the law you order me to be struck?" Those who stood by said, "Would you revile God's high priest?" And Paul said, "I did not know, brethren, that he was the high priest; for it is written, 'You shall not speak evil of a ruler of your people.'"

But when Paul perceived that one part were Sadducees and the other Pharisees, he cried out in the council, "Brethren, I am a Pharisee, a son of Pharisees; with respect to the hope and the resurrection of the dead I am on trial." And when he had said this, a dissension arose between the Pharisees and the Sadducees; and the assembly was divided. For the Sadducees say that there is no resurrection, nor angel, nor spirit; but the Pharisees acknowledge them all. Then a great clamor arose; and some of the scribes of the Pharisees' party stood up and contended, "We find nothing wrong in this man. What if a spirit or an angel spoke to him?" And when the dissension became violent, the tribune, afraid that Paul would be torn in pieces by them, commanded the soldiers to go down and take him by force from among them and bring him into the barracks.

The following night the Lord stood by him and said, "Take courage, for as you have testified about me at Jerusalem, so you must bear witness also at Rome."

After the readings, take a moment of silence to allow the Word to settle into your hearts and to open your heart to the voice of the Holy Spirit.

Personal inspiration:

Sharing

Go around the room and, one by one, share an insight or lesson that was revealed to you from this chapter. (It's OK to pass if desired.)

Personal insights:

Coaching Convo

Is there anyone in the group that needs help applying the lessons from this chapter to a situation in their life? Spend time as a group, using St. Paul's coaching in this chapter, to provide insight into this situation.

Personal struggle:

___

___

___

St. Paul's Condensed Coaching

Many good things don't come to fruition because Flight makes us abandon our efforts before they even begin. St. Paul coaches us that action can be a leader's best friend, and that once we start, God will direct our hearts toward where he wants them to go. We may have to turn around; we may have to change course. But, at least we know that he is walking with us wherever our paths will lead.

"Pondering with Paul" Discussion Questions

Questions are found on p. 115 of the book.

Wrapping Up

Go around the room and, one by one, share an insight or lesson that you'll be taking away from this group conversation. (It's OK to pass if desired.)

> *"No mighty tree of the forest reached its majesty by remaining a seed in the ground. It had to endure the real threats of winds and storms and competition from other trees to reach real heights."*

For Next Time . . .

- Read *Coached by Paul the Apostle* Chapter 7: "In Pain, A Name."
- Reflect on the "Pondering with Paul" questions on page 134.
- Any other group announcements?
- Date, time, and place for the next gathering is ______________________________ .

Closing

Petitions

Members of the group share any petitions that they would like the group to pray for together.

Our Father

Pray the Our Father out loud together, finishing with an appeal to St. Paul:

"St. Paul, pray for us."

EIGHTH GATHERING

Coached by Paul Chapter 7

In Pain, a Name

"*Is the view really worth the climb?*"

Opening Prayer

Choose a volunteer to open the gathering with prayer, either read for the group or from the heart. Prayer for the Year of St. Paul can be found on the inside back cover.

Readings

Choose one to three volunteers to read one or more of the Scriptures below out loud.

1 Corinthians 15:58

Therefore, my beloved brethren, be steadfast, immovable, always abounding in the work of the Lord, knowing that in the Lord your labor is not in vain.

---

2 Corinthians 4:1–18

Therefore, having this ministry by the mercy of God, we do not lose heart. We have renounced disgraceful, underhanded ways; we refuse to practice cunning or to tamper with God's word, but by the open statement of the truth we would commend ourselves to every man's conscience in the sight of God. And even if our gospel is veiled, it is veiled only to those who are perishing. In their case the god of this world has blinded the minds of the unbelievers, to keep them from seeing the light of the gospel of the glory of Christ, who is the likeness of God. For what we preach is not ourselves, but Jesus Christ as Lord, with ourselves as your servants for Jesus' sake. For it is the God who said, "Let light shine out of darkness," who has shone in our hearts to give the light of the knowledge of the glory of God in the face of Christ.

But we have this treasure in earthen vessels, to show that the transcendent power belongs to God and not to us. We are afflicted in every way, but not crushed; perplexed, but not driven to despair; persecuted, but not forsaken; struck down, but not destroyed; always carrying in the body the death of Jesus, so that the life of Jesus may also be manifested in our bodies. For while we live we are always being given up to death for Jesus' sake, so that the life of Jesus may be manifested in our mortal flesh. So death is at work in us, but life in you.

Since we have the same spirit of faith as he had who wrote, "I believed, and so I spoke," we too believe, and so we speak, knowing that he who raised the Lord Jesus will raise us also with Jesus and bring us with you into his presence. For it is all for your sake, so that as grace extends to more and more people it may increase thanksgiving, to the glory of God.

So we do not lose heart. Though our outer nature is wasting away, our inner nature is being renewed every day. For this slight momentary affliction is preparing for us an eternal weight of glory beyond all comparison, because we look not to the things that are seen but to the things that are unseen; for the things that are seen are transient, but the things that are unseen are eternal.

Romans 15:30–33

I appeal to you, brethren, by our Lord Jesus Christ and by the love of the Spirit, to strive together with me in your prayers to God on my behalf, that I may be delivered from the unbelievers in Judea, and that my service for Jerusalem may be acceptable to the saints, so that by God's will I may come to you with joy and be refreshed in your company. The God of peace be with you all. Amen.

After the readings, take a moment of silence to allow the Word to settle into your hearts and to open your heart to the voice of the Holy Spirit.

Personal inspiration:

Sharing

Go around the room and, one by one, share an insight or lesson that was revealed to you from this chapter. (It's OK to pass if desired.)

Personal insights:

Coaching Convo

Is there anyone in the group that needs help applying the lessons from this chapter to a situation in their life? Spend time as a group, using St. Paul's coaching in this chapter, to provide insight into this situation.

Personal struggle:

____

____

____

St. Paul's Condensed Coaching

We encounter fatigue when the doing of things becomes a grind. Things start to feel hard. St. Paul coaches us that being aligned with our identity, with the unique way that God has made us and called us, and remembering that God is pleased with us, our daily grind can be transformed into a prayer that gives glory to God.

"Pondering with Paul" Discussion Questions

Questions are found on p. 134 of the book.

> *"The fact that effectively accomplishing things can be sometimes painful, costing us energy and time that we will never get back, does not have to be viewed as a negative thing."*

Wrapping Up

Go around the room and, one by one, share an insight or lesson that you'll be taking away from this group conversation. (It's OK to pass if desired.)

For Next Time . . .

- Read *Coached by Paul the Apostle* Chapter 8: "In Loss, Gain."
- Reflect on the "Pondering with Paul" questions on page 148.
- Any other group announcements?
- Date, time, and place for the next gathering is ______________________________.

Closing

Petitions

Members of the group share any petitions that they would like the group to pray for together.

Our Father

Pray the Our Father out loud together, finishing with an appeal to St. Paul:

"St. Paul, pray for us."

"We literally become ourselves more and more by choosing to act in accord with God's love…"

NINTH GATHERING

Coached by Paul Chapter 8

In Loss, Gain

> *"For many, suffering is a problem to be solved instead of a necessity to be embraced as we pursue something greater."*

Opening Prayer

Choose a volunteer to open the gathering with prayer, either read for the group or from the heart. Prayer for the Year of St. Paul can be found on the inside back cover.

Readings

Choose one to three volunteers to read one or more of the Scriptures below out loud.

Philippians 3:12–21

Not that I have already obtained this or am already perfect; but I press on to make it my own, because Christ Jesus has made me his own. Brethren, I do not consider that I have made it my own; but one thing I do, forgetting what lies behind and straining forward to what lies ahead, I press on toward the goal for the prize of the upward call of God in Christ Jesus. Let those of us who are mature be thus minded; and if in anything you are otherwise minded, God will reveal that also to you. Only let us hold true to what we have attained.

Brethren, join in imitating me, and mark those who so live as you have an example in us. For many, of whom I have often told you and now tell you even with tears, live as enemies of the cross of Christ. Their end is destruction, their god is the belly, and they glory in their shame, with minds set on earthly things. But our commonwealth is in heaven, and from it we await a Savior, the Lord Jesus Christ, who will change our lowly body to be like his glorious body, by the power which enables him even to subject all things to himself.

---

2 Timothy 4:1–8

I charge you in the presence of God and of Christ Jesus who is to judge the living and the dead, and by his appearing and his kingdom: preach the word, be urgent in season and out of season, convince, rebuke, and exhort, be unfailing in patience and in teaching. For the time is coming when people will not endure sound teaching, but having itching ears they will accumulate for themselves teachers to suit their own likings, and will turn away from listening to the truth and wander into myths. As for you, always be steady, endure suffering, do the work of an evangelist, fulfil your ministry.

For I am already on the point of being sacrificed; the time of my departure has come. I have fought the good fight, I have finished the race, I have kept the faith. Henceforth there is laid up for me the crown of righteousness, which the Lord, the righteous judge, will award to me on that Day, and not only to me but also to all who have loved his appearing.

---

2 Timothy 1:1–5

Paul, an apostle of Christ Jesus by the will of God according to the promise of the life which is in Christ Jesus,

To Timothy, my beloved child:

Grace, mercy, and peace from God the Father and Christ Jesus our Lord.

I thank God whom I serve with a clear conscience, as did my fathers, when I remember you constantly in my prayers. As I remember your tears, I long night and day to see you, that I may be filled with joy. I am reminded of your sincere faith, a faith that dwelt first in your grandmother Lois and your mother Eunice and now, I am sure, dwells in you.

After the readings, take a moment of silence to allow the Word to settle into your hearts and to open your heart to the voice of the Holy Spirit.

Personal inspiration:

Sharing

Go around the room and, one by one, share an insight or lesson that was revealed to you from this chapter. (It's OK to pass if desired.)

Personal insights:

Coaching Convo

Is there anyone in the group that needs help applying the lessons from this chapter to a situation in their life? Spend time as a group, using St. Paul's coaching in this chapter, to provide insight into this situation.

Personal struggle:

____

____

____

St. Paul's Condensed Coaching

Fatigue can set in when the perseverance of our labors are not aligned with the goals we are motivated to achieve. St. Paul coaches us that the love of the Lord which burns in our hearts is a well of perseverance that Christ offers to help us run the race. Just like Paul, we need to open our eyes to the wonderful things God is doing through our efforts, celebrate them, and continue forward.

"Pondering with Paul" Discussion Questions

Questions are found on p. 148 of the book.

> *"Hupomoné: the ability to "stand underneath" the weight of our challenges and pay the price of victory by enduring the pain it will require."*

Wrapping Up

Go around the room and, one by one, share an insight or lesson that you'll be taking away from this group conversation. (It's OK to pass if desired.)

For Next Time . . .

- Read *Coached by Paul the Apostle* Chapter 9: "In Solitude, Friends."
- Reflect on the "Pondering with Paul" questions on page 163.
- Any other group announcements?
- Date, time, and place for the next gathering is
  ____ .

Closing

Petitions

Members of the group share any petitions that they would like the group to pray for together.

Our Father

Pray the Our Father out loud together, finishing with an appeal to St. Paul:

"St. Paul, pray for us."

". . . love can reach its goal even when our efforts fail."

TENTH GATHERING

Coached by Paul Chapter 9

In Solitude, Friends

"Like the prow of a ship, a leader has to break the waves and the ice of their ship's chosen course for the sake of those who will sail gently in the wake their efforts leave behind."

Opening Prayer

Choose a volunteer to open the gathering with prayer, either read for the group or from the heart. Prayer for the Year of St. Paul can be found on the inside back cover.

Readings

Choose one to three volunteers to read one or more of the Scriptures below out loud.

2 Corinthians 10:1–18

I, Paul, myself entreat you, by the meekness and gentleness of Christ—I who am humble when face to face with you, but bold to you when I am away!—I beg of you that when I am present I may not have to show boldness with such confidence as I count on showing against some who suspect us of acting in worldly fashion. For though we live in the world we are not carrying on a worldly war, for the weapons of our warfare are not worldly but have divine power to destroy strongholds. We destroy arguments and every proud obstacle to the knowledge of God, and take every thought captive to obey Christ, being ready to punish every disobedience, when your obedience is complete.

Look at what is before your eyes. If any one is confident that he is Christ's, let him remind himself that as he is Christ's, so are we. For even if I boast a little too much of our authority, which the Lord gave for building you up and not for destroying you, I shall not be put to shame. I would not seem to be frightening you with letters. For they say, "His letters are weighty and strong, but his bodily presence is weak, and his speech of no account." Let such people understand that what we say by letter when absent, we do when present. Not that we venture to class or compare ourselves with some of those who commend themselves. But when they measure themselves by one another, and compare themselves with one another, they are without understanding.

But we will not boast beyond limit, but will keep to the limits God has apportioned us, to reach even to you. For we are not overextending ourselves, as though we did not reach you; we were the first to come all the way to you with the gospel of Christ. We do not boast beyond limit, in other men's labors; but our hope is that as your faith increases, our field among you may be greatly enlarged, so that we may preach the gospel in lands beyond you, without boasting of work already done in another's field. "Let him who boasts, boast of the Lord." For it is not the man who commends himself that is accepted, but the man whom the Lord commends.

Philippians 3:1–11
Finally, my brethren, rejoice in the Lord. To write the same things to you is not irksome to me, and is safe for you.

Look out for the dogs, look out for the evil-workers, look out for those who mutilate the flesh. For we are the true circumcision, who worship God in spirit, and glory in Christ

Jesus, and put no confidence in the flesh. Though I myself have reason for confidence in the flesh also. If any other man thinks he has reason for confidence in the flesh, I have more: circumcised on the eighth day, of the people of Israel, of the tribe of Benjamin, a Hebrew born of Hebrews; as to the law a Pharisee, as to zeal a persecutor of the church, as to righteousness under the law blameless. But whatever gain I had, I counted as loss for the sake of Christ. Indeed I count everything as loss because of the surpassing worth of knowing Christ Jesus my Lord. For his sake I have suffered the loss of all things, and count them as refuse, in order that I may gain Christ and be found in him, not having a righteousness of my own, based on law, but that which is through faith in Christ, the righteousness from God that depends on faith; that I may know him and the power of his resurrection, and may share his sufferings, becoming like him in his death, that if possible I may attain the resurrection from the dead.

---

1 Corinthians 4:8–13
Already you are filled! Already you have become rich! Without us you have become kings! And would that you did reign, so that we might share the rule with you! For I think that God has exhibited us apostles as last of all, like men sentenced to death; because we have become a spectacle to the world, to angels and to men. We are fools for Christ's sake, but you are wise in Christ. We are weak, but you are strong. You are

held in honor, but we in disrepute. To the present hour we hunger and thirst, we are ill-clad and buffeted and homeless, and we labor, working with our own hands. When reviled, we bless; when persecuted, we endure; when slandered, we try to conciliate; we have become, and are now, as the refuse of the world, the offscouring of all things.

After the readings, take a moment of silence to allow the Word to settle into your hearts and to open your heart to the voice of the Holy Spirit.

Personal inspiration:

Sharing

Go around the room and, one by one, share an insight or lesson that was revealed to you from this chapter. (It's OK to pass if desired.)

Personal insights:

Coaching Convo

Is there anyone in the group that needs help applying the lessons from this chapter to a situation in their life? Spend time as a group, using St. Paul's coaching in this chapter, to provide insight into this situation.

Personal struggle:

St. Paul's Condensed Coaching

Forlornness prevents us from sharing with others what we have done, and so they can never be a part of it. Paul coaches us that, despite weakness and embarrassment, we can serve God with our whole heart, knowing that we will never stand alone as long as Christ is in our hearts. He is with us, always.

"Pondering with Paul" Discussion Questions

Questions are found on p. 163 of the book.

> *"[St. Paul] followed Christ repeatedly into positions of weakness, subservience, and even embarrassment, and then he served him there with his whole heart."*

Wrapping Up

Go around the room and, one by one, share an insight or lesson that you'll be taking away from this group conversation. (It's OK to pass if desired.)

For Next Time . . .

- Read *Coached by Paul the Apostle* Chapter 10: "Life on the Edge."
- Any other group announcements?
- Date, time, and place for the next gathering is ______________________________.

Closing

Petitions

Members of the group share any petitions that they would like the group to pray for together.

Our Father

Pray the Our Father out loud together, finishing with an appeal to St. Paul:

"St. Paul, pray for us."

"Rising to lead means standing to be judged."

ELEVENTH GATHERING

Coached by Paul Chapter 10

Life on the Edge

"He felt the power of Christian Courage that sees in every obstacle to love an opportunity for Christ's power to flow through us."

Opening Prayer

Choose a volunteer to open the gathering with prayer, either read for the group or from the heart. Prayer for the Year of St. Paul can be found on the inside back cover.

Readings

Choose one volunteer to read the Scripture below out loud.

2 Timothy 4:6–8

For I am already on the point of being sacrificed; the time of my departure has come. I have fought the good fight, I have finished the race, I have kept the faith. Henceforth there is laid up for me the crown of righteousness, which the Lord, the righteous judge, will award to me on that Day, and not only to me but also to all who have loved his appearing.

After the readings, take a moment of silence to allow the Word to settle into your hearts and to open your heart to the voice of the Holy Spirit.

Personal inspiration:

Sharing

Go around the room and, one by one, share an insight or lesson that was revealed to you from this chapter. (It's OK to pass if desired.)

Personal insights:

____

____

____

Coaching Convo

Is there anyone in the group that needs help applying the lessons from this chapter to a situation in their life? Spend time as a group, using St. Paul's coaching in this chapter, to provide insight into this situation.

Personal struggle:

____

____

____

St. Paul's Condensed Coaching

Daring great things for Christ was the central fire that burned in Paul's heart. He leaves us an example of zeal for God that is captivating and compelling. Acting with Christian Courage allowed Paul to tread boldly in the footsteps of Christ and make a true difference in his world. By his grace, God can do the same in ours.

Wrapping Up

Go around the room and, one by one, share an insight or lesson that you'll be taking away from St. Paul's coaching. (It's OK to pass if desired.)

Closing

Petitions

Members of the group share any petitions that they would like the group to pray for together.

Our Father

Pray the Our Father out loud together, finishing with an appeal to St. Paul:

"St. Paul, pray for us."

Notes

Notes

Congratulations

on spending eleven gatherings being coached by St. Paul! We hope that, through fellowship with each other and with this great saint, you've grown closer to the Father through Christ by the power of the Holy Spirit. You are in our prayers here at the Saint John Institute.

Join our "Coached!" community by sharing a picture of your group with us to showcase on our website, daregreatthings.org. Send us an email at dgt@saintjohninstitute.org or use the hashtag #CoachedbyPaul on social media.

Thank you for sharing this journey with us! If you'd like to continue to "dare great things for Christ," learn about our in-person and online events at saintjohninstitute.org and daregreatthings.org.

About the Saint John Institute

The Saint John Institute strives to raise up saints to lead by bringing the power of faith to leadership and the power of leadership to faith. Forging a vision for Christian leadership through its unique AUDEO Approach™, the Saint John Institute offers programs across the country for leaders in business, spouses, parents, and leaders in culture, through retreats, workshops, classes, and online content, including its podcast "Dare Great Things for Christ." In addition to inspiring retreats, skills training, and personal leadership development, the Saint John Institute proudly partners with businesses and organizations to provide customized leadership development and cultural transformation. The Saint John Institute is a non-profit organization.

Here are some ways to get involved with the Saint John Institute:

- Listen to our podcast, "Dare Great Things for Christ," on your favorite app or podcast streaming service.
- Join the Saint John Leadership Network at saintjohninstitute.org/saint-john-leadership-network/.
- Donate to the Saint John Institute at saintjohninstitute.org/donate/.
- Become a business partner of the Saint John Institute at saintjohninstitute.org/saint-john-leadership-network/becoming-a-corporate-partner/.
- Check out our in-person events at saintjohninstitute.org/sji-events/.
- Go deeper with online leadership courses available at daregreatthings.org.